Encanta

POETRY DE ENCANTA

ALBERT NYANGARESI

TABLE OF CONTENTS

Poetry De Encanta

By Albert Nyangaresi

Copyright page

Copyright(C)Albert Nyangaresi
Country Kenya ◈ ◈
Year of publishing 2024

Acknowledgment

I would like to extend my heartfelt gratitude to the following individuals and organizations for their invaluable support in the creation of this poetry book, "De Encanta."

First and foremost, I am deeply grateful to the Poetry Club at MaasaiMara University for their encouragement and guidance throughout my journey as a poet. Their belief in my work has been a constant source of inspiration.

I would also like to express my sincere appreciation to TibezAlbershile, AlbertoKelly, and Tiberius Alberto, who played a significant role in helping me shape and refine the poems in this collection. Their insightful suggestions and constructive feedback were instrumental in bringing "De Encanta" to life.

This book would not have been possible without the support of these wonderful individuals and the Poetry Club at MaasaiMara University. I am honored to have had the opportunity to share my poetry with them, and I am grateful for their unwavering encouragement and mentorship.

Thank you all for your kindness, and dedication. I am truly fortunate to have had the chance to work with such talented and supportive individuals.

Sincerely,

Albert Nyangaresi Mokera

Introduction

Welcome poetry De Encanta," a collection of poems that explores the depths of the human experience. This book is a labor of love, crafted with passion and dedication, and it is my sincere hope that it will touch the hearts and minds of my readers.

As a poet, I have always been fascinated by the power of words to evoke emotions, paint vivid images, and convey complex ideas. Through my poems, I aim to transport my readers to different worlds, them feel, think, and reflect.

The poems in "De Encanta" are a reflection of my own experiences, observations, and musings. They are a celebration of life, love, nature, and the beauty of the human spirit. Each poem is a unique journey, a exploration of the depths of the human experience, and I am proud to share them with you.

I am grateful to have had the opportunity to work with an incredible team of individuals who have supported me throughout my journey as a poet. Their encouragement, guidance, and feedback have been invaluable, and I am honored to acknowledge their contributions in the acknowledgment page.

I hope that "Poetry De Encanta" will inspire, provoke, and delight you. Whether you are a fellow poet, a literature enthusiast, or simply someone who appreciates the beauty of words,

I am confident that these poems will resonate with you on a deep and.

Thank you for joining me on this poetic journey. I am humbled and grateful to have had the chance to share my work with you, and I hope that " poetry De Encanta" will leave a lasting impression on your heart and mind.

Sincerely,
Albert Nyangaresi Mokera

"Poetry De Encanta" by Albert Nyangaresi is a captivating collection of poems that will transport readers to a world of beauty, passion, and introspection. Nyangaresi's words are like magic, weaving a spell that enchants and inspires. The poems are rich in imagery and emotion, making them a true delight for readers of all ages.

From the opening pages, it's clear that Nyangaresi is a masterful wordsmith, using language to paint vivid pictures in the reader's mind. The poems are diverse in theme, ranging from love and relationships to nature and self-discovery. Each poem is a unique gem, offering something special to every reader.

One of the standout features of "Poetry De Encanta" is its ability to evoke powerful emotions in the reader. Nyangaresi's words have a way of touching the heart, making this book a must-read for anyone who appreciates poetry that resonates on a deep level.

Overall, "Poetry De Encanta" is a stunning collection of poems that showcases Albert Nyangaresi's talent and creativity. It is a true gem in the world of literature, and I highly recommend it to anyone who, emotive, and thought-provoking poetry.

1. Encanta

"Encanta "
Actually is one and only quarantine l just have my heart
I don't think of the others in each country of continents
I can't even which girl wiii wonna match with her
Her scent can make you have a sweet sleep
Surely is one in a million many my think they can out smart her but they are doing zero zone work
Some are speaking ill towards her teasing her to end our relationship
What actually they receive more passionate even can't reason of such foolish plan's
Simplicity is her identity in every steps of life
Actually l wonder if it's a dream on sun day
Actually her name kelcys has given me hope to see future
She has taken the Keys of my heart ooooooh
I don't know who can steal them from my kelcys
Many is a suprise of how is my heart
They know am shy speaking in speaking
They forget that speaking and writing are different things
What l fear in this life is losing her from my hearto I never thought of anybody whom can be loyal as my lovingly heart
I can say ,sing even write
million writing just for her alone and only
Composed by Albershile tibez

2. Alone

"Alone"

No friend for me
Me alone in the world
World of wonders
So sorry to say
No one to call
Nor madre nor hermano
All home no no
Why why to me
Alone alone rom everyone
Let my lonely be pillar
Time wiii definitely tell
My lonely was with meaning
All lonely for lonely
Even my heart isnt
Fake friends are dangerous
Smart in playing
What did l do
Lonely yet not alone
My favourite father
My giver and my sustainer Always support me
So no more lonely
Patients pay
Indeed l gonna try
No more on
This world friendship
Only l gonna friend
My creator
Surely indeed
No more worries

Creativity of centuries
I gonna have
Alone alone
Amazing and universe
Gonna dance to my tunes
No more of this lonely
Comfort from my father
I feel far from my life
Am paradise praying And dancing to sweet
Sounds and melodies
Composed by Tibez Albershile

3. Changes

"Changes"
Time change as chameleon changes its colours
Today we are firm as affirmative tomorrow on farm it's over
So painful yet you were so patient and humble
So sorry to say to people on sad story you experienced
So happy to be in a relationship to sorry to know you are just nothing
Why do we allow chameleon in our relationship
So hurt breaking to by loyal in name of love tomorrow you are alone in tears
So complex to say today is my sweetheart soulmate but tomorrow is shift with someone
Why can't we be serious even once as sun and rain I wonder as wondering Jew on summary sun day
Where when did all occurred in my life story
What was the hidden mistry that has been revealed right now
Am worried without any answer whom can l ask
All l know aren't with me today they flew away leaving me back
Am surprised actually when all the Changes wiii be erased completely
Myself am a dormant volcano without any say to satution
Composed by Tiberius Alberto

4. Climax

" Climax"
    So sad to say byeeeeeee
    Those who have been with you
    So sorry to see that happening no need to tell
    Every event has it's own reasons right or wrong
    We thought it can be coldwell
    Yet all of you are wrong l wonder
    Why nature to be unfair such as this that make me cry
    Crying can't change fact
    The fact wiii be seen soon
    No where to hide my head my face from Facebook
    His statement suprise me so much
    Where to start where to end
    It's just a text but leave me to tense and tear's
    I run but l found l same room
    Where to run l don't know keeping in mind soon wiii be over
    I worry why Tibez transfer his territory but l just seeing some reason
    Surely nothing in the earth is hidden below the sun Let me see the sunlight shinny toward the solar panels
    Waiting what tomorrow , might bring in.
    Composed by:Tibez Albershile

5. Love

"Love"

His love is loyal as the sand of the sea

We may hurt him so deeply but no day he can give up on us

His love shelters even the sinner's

His praise makes world be at peace

His understanding is above our underestimation

What we see impossible is possible to him

Day in out no matter how much his good deeds are dead in eyes and heart we can't see

Our sins have acted as obstacles on seeing his love and light

His light is all over the cosmos yet being careless can't see

Some time l think but my thoughts are thoughtless

How can we understand is the source of soul and life

We are nothing infront of his eyes each day we are able to see due to his love So painful sorrow to whom we hear yet we are ignorant indeed we are inviting our destruction

Composed by Albert nyangaresi

6. Crop

" Crop'

Actually l am so happy honesty

Seeing what back days l thought was simple to be serious

Actually l have seen a new crop being bought from market

Marking a new beginning hopefully the new crop wiii not disappoint farmer's farm

I never thought of a day of seeing the crop in selling centre

The crop already as l see from previous history it's so painful in one's farm

But because l have no say let's wait to see this season

Maybe it can change and we see it so productive

Only God knows we are simple being it's so hard to know

Am only worried about farmer since the only small things he has it's the farm

The family also are waiting to harvest heavily from new crop

Bad luck is that the crop don't do much in such area and farmer isn't aware

I wonder why did he chose this crop actually l have no answer l am waiting wanting to see

Composed by Tiberius Alberto

7. Dreams

"Dreams

When a child is born parents wish great things

No parent may wish to see his child in problem regardless

The child start his life with his mother as her teacher

Next level the child also move to higher education level the school where character is formed

Where the child make new friends and meet new fellow's

There studies start with aim of each child making her mother proud

As life is full of ups and downs the one who sacrifices succeed in next level

Where the dreams are starting to accommodate in the mind many are good

The child wonder which to choose but with trust

One who trust God in every step definitely end up succeeding

Move to next level of placing his dreams to particular levels of world

With all one is able to fulfill his family dreams and placing his family to sky

Composed by Albert nyangaresi

8. Ex

"Ex"

When l look, at my life l wonder
What did l do to her,to insult me heartlesly,
I gave her my heart , body and soul return l receive heartbreak,
My sweet messages, now aren't of meaning,
I have turned useless, as slippers on her eyes,
I wish even l can trace , a tunnel underground and hide ,
She has turned ,completely scorpion in my life,
My mind is full of million , questions without any answer,
I am deeply hurt by her directly attack, like a fighter in war field,
How can l wipe, my feelings from her,
Sweet memories, are hunting me when l recall how l was arrogant to my master,
Am speechless ,seeing my satution today ,
I can't believe , that despite how dedicated l was l am alone today
I feel like finding a place , far from her and stay ,
Starting a new, lifestyle so simple near the sea,
I can be relieved, from her hands and heart ,
I pray to almighty, God since is all knowing,
Why to suffer, why my chapter can't be closed,
All l found ,no answer l only leave to my father,
Actually she took ,my simplicity for granted ,
She flew away as an emergency flight
I feel to fall to a sleep, slowly and found my father ,l dedicate only my life to him alone ,
So painful ,story to say to someone
Composed by Albert nyangaresi

9. Fine

"Fine "

So cute l feel free from my stress

For sure she has taken my heart my beautiful angel

I don't think someone else a part from you my love

Surely l have again fallen in love in her love

I don't even think of anything else l feel just looking to her beautiful face from morning till night

I don't know what phrase l gonna use to impress her My heart has already accepted her without any worries

The way she smile l feel l have seen a shining machine

That gonna enlight my life with virtues and everything to attain success

Am ready on her cage just by swee scent of her smell

The way she holds me l feel holding her from morning till end of time

Actually Tiberius has discovered definition of love that gonna teach

Her name Joan make begun of success story of Tiberius

Composed by Tiberius Alberto

10. Friends

"Friends"
  Whom can l call ,a friend am wondering ,as wonder woman,
  Who is a friend , real friend not an imaginary friend like image,
  Why can't l see ,whom to call a friend for sure ,
  Many are good ,in greeting but does it make you my friend ,
  Am tired ,of pretenders liars my life is sweet as sugar,
  Yet are ready to enter, and manipulate my simplicity,
  All in the name ,of friend are you my friend ,
  Am worried, which friend that betrayal me with my enemies ,
  A friend whom, is there chewing my only one cash from the cashier,
  I wonder ,whom ready to give me out for sake of superiority,
  Whom can l shout, out to tell is my true friend,
  It's that gives me, alcohol to be drunk and do all that he likes with my
body ,
  Whom is my friend, where to search my sweet true friend for me,
  What mistake ,did l do l received only disappointment,
  My simple slow ,lifestyle hasn't affected anybody,
  Why then, l receive irony of what expected,
  So painful to pay ,attention to such liars ,
  Am worried, when wiii l find my friend whom ,
  Am sure we gonna share same experience
  Composed by Albert nyangaresi.

11. Gift

"Gift "

My heart you are my world whom complete me
I don't think of anything else a part from our success
I feel saying l love you alot
Bad luck l found myself speechless looking to your
Simple eyes which l have already sin my love actually
Your simplicity l wonder can l found a girl like you this century
You are my gift that almighty granted to be next with me
I feel to Compose million poetic poems for her
Her heart has actually accepted my invitation
When looking careful to her eyes l see eternity binding
Which l don't think of anyone gonna break if not almighty
Whom has granted us gift of life and love as gift to demonstrate
Day in and out l am trying to hide from my heart but where
I gonna hide actually all the keys and password she has taken
This time Tiberius Alberto has definitely found a treasure
That gonna stay with her and also of same character
Am lark withness of this love actually none ever thought of Tiberius
Alberto loving again
Only was by God wiii and Joan pretty made Tiberius statue
On looking to her pretty she made Tiberius to purelize his heart to
avoid disappointment Composed by Albert Nyangaresi

12. Happy

" happy"
    Sing sing
    From days to weeks
    Weeks to months
    We have been waiting
    The day to come
    Day of joy
    Each family for
    This day every one
    Estas feliz
    No more of enemies
    Story of people
    We used to see
    Society is save
    This day from Morning tii nouche
    It's joy joy
    Melodies of love
    In deed what has
    Start has end
    Year we saw
    Full of challenges
    Christ has taken away all
    This day from every minute
    We speak we feel for sure
    We aren't the same we are
    Different from the past years
    As lighting we are matching
    Towards nuevo anos
    We are optimistic of
    Million things

Year of success
For we have started
With him and we gonna
Come to climax with him
Many in number
Wished to see this day
Yet are five feet down
The ground this indeed
Is one of your mercy my
Eyes are small but 1
Can see million of things
All as per your wiii
Indeed we owe you
Composed by Tibez Albershile

13. Heart

"Heart"

Mi Skylark mi, Moonlight, Tu eres Encanta ,estas mucho ,
Let them say it,you are Tibez
Heart,
Fear nothing ,forever in Tibez,
Take me step by step, see future, We gonna create, together carefully,
Next to me ,my Amor Tu eres Tibez,
Estas feliz ,en esta journey de Encanta,
I wanna hear, only from my Amor,
She is indeed amazing, when did Tibez,
Manage to get, girl like her ,
I can't believe, she is so beautiful,
I don't think l gonna , get my eyes,
Out of her , I feel to be given her ,
As a regalo right ,from start of story,
However Tibez can't , leave her come,
Rain or fire the lady, l wonder if was ,
Caught in capture re capture,by Tibez,
No cant happen , I think the lady loves,
Our friend alot , the glittering face,
It's a clear indication , our brother Tibez,
For first time, gonna end the shly ,
Yeah Tibez gonna end , the child's deed,
I only think the mountains, and valleys,
Wiii Tibez manage, only time gonna tell,
No time we know well him , no girlfriend,
Tibez has ever had in the lifetime, we just
Hopefully for best, our amigo,
Now gonna feel warm,wow amazing,

Who thought,who expected from Tibez, This indeed is peer pressure, no no

This is Tibez ,who l know, full of love,

Melodies in writing and reality ,

Bravo Tibez ,black chocolatecunning,

She took Tibez, middle in hight so cute, Calling her Amor, Tibez didn't make mistake, Love is full of many things, we see skin,

We don't see heart, Tibez is other level,

We agree or not agree, l see smile,

For decades did day, surely Tibez got a teacher,

For the topic where is weak, love is bond see mi amigos,

The love the two share, story is taking another level,

Call her heart of Tibez , Skylark that give our migo sleepless nights,

From the lifestyle of Tibez, we gonna see many in this world,

Composed by Tibez Albershile

14. Lifestyle

"Lifestyle"

Why worries to overload my mind
Can't they erased or removed every time
No l have to stop my self
Memories and melodies can't control my lifestyle
Betrayal can't make me fail
My success l have struggle from grass to graze I can't imagine of failure in my future for love What can l say to my mentor , master
That can't happen regardless am still strong
My dreams to be great tiii end of time
Just be ruined by a simple hurtbreak l cat imagine
Can l sustain such life better to die day time
Than watching my hard work going to waste
Lifetime l have learnt many million
Which some are positive others are negative nevertheless why am still
Firm as future no matter how complex it's we continue fighting
My simplicity lifestyle could have been swept away
My title in society was sent away as simple as a b c
My lifestyle Is so sweet of good memories of my success
Composed by Albert nyangaresi

15. Machine

"Machine"
The shining machine made me statue
Just by the look of view of outside appearance
Yet l haven't know even the elements of machine
But it might be ligit and long lasting thing
Hopefully my dollars l gonna invest wiii be of sense surely
I feel to know it's actually operations in my daily basis activities
Hopefully no difference it gonna make with my team
Since l am not ready to lose any one of my team themly new character
So I have to be careful as class of scientific research
My mind is full of preguntas on new machine
The glittery make me a bit surprised satutionary
So in simple as subject submission
I was left with no option from taking the commodity to my residence region
The fear of the cunning malicious gonna make me afraid
What l gonna put in place for its security purpose
Am worried as a working farmer without fruit actually
Where to locate it in my palace of many priceless commodities
What mechanism l wiii place for now and future safety
I am left without any answer at all
The way is so delicate as digital computers
I can't afford to see my pounds go to waste at all
Composed by Tiberius Alberto

16. Memories

"Memories "

Time has passed as fast as lighting all my past stories are there

Where did l mess up with an my only love whom was so dedicated day in out

Am worried actually no more of her daily basis call no sweet words like honey

They have been past stories and now everything is starting

I wonder as wondering Jew whom can l replace her with this century love is chameleon

Only memories and melodies of her on my mind

My heart is hurt completely l don't know where to start again

I don't think of any love anymore l feel hated deep down my heart

What pain me most is sweet words of betrayal

Make me in tier's actually l can't erase the dark side she created in my life

All my friends aren't with me all flew away as results of her

Am alone with my God whom never disappoint anyone

Painful story is when recalling false promises day time

Only death can act as barrier to our love story I remain statue

Sweetness that sounds good but so dangerous

Surely l conquer not all glitters is gold

She even thought me definition of love but was defined to leave me alone

Why and when all this sorrows started from l wonder

Composed by Tiberius Alberto

17. Mistake

"Mistake"
Maybe my mind is wrong
Why when I see my plans succeeding end up to worst
When will I see her my only loyal love
Or did I make a mistake making her my heart
Am left without any answer
My time my efforts I have to dedicate to my Amor
Nature grant me many milion chances I can not blame it
Let me listen to my heart before my next step
My heart is attached to her so is my queen
I have to come with something like standard timetable
Since she is my only one and true love
Am compel to think beyond the box
Coming out with best plan since surrendering isn't my phrase
Tomorrow I need to think and think best solution
Actually Tiberius isn't know of failure
Tell me all you wish but not to fail
My amor time has challenged me
But never shake we are together tiii
Eternity let them say what they feel
You are my missing piece of my life
Your love from start tiii end I am statue
No one gonna be like you my love
Joan this journey is so complex
Yet your support I see success
No more of worries of anything
All mistake aren't it's nuevo anos
Means nuevo stories of Encanta
See mi la novia what they wanna
Do to blame me yet you are with me

So surprising my Skylark
Composed by Tibez Albershile

18. Mmarau

"Mmarau"

We have actually, arrived home far from home,

Where many we have been, waiting for,

A home to write our academic, stories from start to end,

We believe in spirit, our dreams day in out wiii be fulfilled,

The warm welcome,we have received as mother and child,

We feel to shout to universe,to see the love of our lectures,

The are eagerly to impact knowledge, to us to be key to society in various forms,

The program in place,are so inspiring to see success,

Like other institutions also, mmarau has motto that inspires alot,

When one is going astray,the motto act as his mentor,

A part from programs,the institution has avail internet,

For online learning and encourage learner, to do more on field of research,

The library also is available for those ready to explore,more in various fields for success,

The environment is so touching, to allow one to take studies peaceful

,

The security is on day and night to assure student are secure to fullfil their dreams, The security department ,also ensure off-campus security for good mentality and focus in academic,

Surely we can't say, that there is a good institution like mmarau in academic success,

And the institution believe, that with grace of God all impossible is possible,

Making maasai mara university,a God fearing institution,

Sky might be limit, success is assured in mmarau, Composed by Tiberius Alberto ,,

19. Migos

"Migos"
    Tell me more and more, It's interesante to hear, Call friend from far,
    To party for our dinero,
    Am now full of pesos,
    I wanna to work things,
    So mi amigos gonna, Feel paradise particular,
    To this event of evening.
    Call all the ladies, You wanna have ,
    All are for you ,
    Remember to be careful,
    On today actions for ,
    The welfare of tomorrow,
    Why to tell you ,
    Yet you know,
    It's because you,
    Are mi amigos,
    And that what amigos,
    Do to fellow Migos.
    Make more fun,
    See the funny,
    Girl from far,
    She look so cute, Amazing indeed,
    Not all glitter is gold,
    Yet she is my sunshine,
    When wiii we reach to ,
    Hear and I talk to her,
    I feel to be feed,
    By her love .
    Migos Migos,
    Esta dai esta dai,

Enjoy everything,
Feel yourself,
Maybe this is ,
Last chance on line, So try to use to fullest, Why memories more,
Daily basis do they,
Come to mind,
Am completely,
Hurt wiii day,
All be over melodies,
More touching.
Fake friends for real,
Forced made me,
To enter to a un wanted,
Universe to meet ,
My destruction to,
Touching to hear to,
Call friend call to ,
Satan to speak to, Such liars day to ,
Today to our story.
Composed by Tibez Albershile

20. Player

"player"

Sun set settings ,my mind to cool on busy day, I pray day in out that, what l see wasn't reality reason,

I can not manage, this life of of competition of love ,

Yet myself am not a player, how wiii l manage this football field,

My hands are ready ,to surrender so shifty,

When to come to players, even l do not know how to play,

Yet she wants ,l to enter the field ,

Tibez l do not think ,so actually how l gonna do it,

My lifestyle l prefer ,so humble and so simplicity lifestyle,

Making me player, even my principles gonna go away,

And l will be statue to just watch,

Without principles l do not know,how l gonna stay so painful but l can not be a player , Let if rain come, l wii be so firm as affirmative with my rules, l am simple as a,b ,c with, for the satution hopefully tomorrow wiii be so good,

Let l pray not to be played ,in this game of love,

So as l wiii not be lost ,as Barbel in the holy scriptures,

For that l pray to avoid ,to be a player or being played as futbol game,

I only thank almighty ,to grant greater view on the game , Sure l would have been, in tear's today and even tomorrow,

With that l think ,to seek a prayerful partner not player one ,

Which inspires me to search Christian and hopefully life,

Composed by: Tiberius Alberto

21. Minutes

"Minutes"
Sunshine to my bird
She is my moonlight The memories might
Freeze me but melodies
Of her wii indeed kill
Me my favourite one
I don't know when
Wiii l see my bird
That make me to
Feel eternal bond
Am tired of watching
I wanna my bird
I wanna we go
Suck nectar together
See my nest my Amor
I wanna we gonna be
We alone to this journey
I don't think l gonna do
Anything a part from
Seeing mi bird in my
Nest we gonna disfruta
Contigo from day to day
My bird am waiting
For your signal
For the joy epic
Journey we wiii
Be together tiii
Eternity no more
Of other spices
Only we alone

In the universe
Full of sweet melodies
Of love from time to time
Minutes wiii soon send Us away to chiling
Zone more sad
Story to hear
I gut only few
Seconds now Sun is setting From the look
Yet l haven't said
To my bird my feelings
My bird l fear to say it
I am worried wiii
My bird go with my
Game go go
No no no
Yet my game goes
On the sun is not
Anymore
From weeks to days
Days to hours how
Things went hours
To minutes minutes
No no no
Minutes to seconds Seconds to microseconds
So touching to hear
No say say
Wiii the bird go
Who knows the bird
Composed by Tibez Albershile
22.valantine
"Valantine"
Bell baile melodies ,

What a day who expected,
We gonna reach today my,
Skylark we have gone miles,
Together as unit mi amor,
Today l wanna say to universe,
To hear this she is mi ,
Valantine no other, She gives me love,
You love am lost,
My sweetheart my valantine,
Shine little they see honey,
Surely l gonna lick, Your love slowly ,
I don't wish to see ,
Interference for my step,
I wanna lick it slowly ,
Just as little bebe trying,
A walk l wiii be happy,
Man this valantine ,
By the look of eyes,
I see paradise my amor,
Cuteness overloading,
My beb l wanna ,
We gonna go on ,
A trip to see your,
Suprise for esta dai,
I wanna you feel love,
My love this day my amor ,
You feel eternal bond mi Amor,
Just l can't imagine love,
You gut me my love,
What a day melodies,
My favourite song so ,
Amazing l never thought,

You gonna gut me so deep,
I really feel feliz con mi Amor,
Slowly slowly dancing, Morning tiii nouche,
Love songs of our century,
What l gonna say,
Indeed my valantine ,
It's one in a million ,
Composed by Tibez Albershile

23. Maa

"Maa"
The love lesson
They give me my
Mind I don't mind
The black basic
Nature of them
Gonna fade from
Me mental picture In my mind I will
Erase it
The beauty necks
Make me stare
A little what l gonna
Say the melodies
Of the maa songs
Has turned to my
Santuri so amazing
Whom gonna gaze
That Tibez gonna
Feel feliz contigo
Maa society
Wow wow the
Culture aspect
Good guidance
To youths in the
Earlier life has
Made the society to grow
The maa society
Custom continually
Has influence many
To explore the maa land

The breeze before
Reaching maa land
Welcome one warmly
This can make one see
Sense that has reached
Paradise yet person
Is not paradise it's maa
That is welcoming wow
Can't wait to see to listen
To songs and dance Like one of the Maa Member I wanna
Teaste the maa
Culture
The culture which
Has been and yet to be
Full of rules running the
Community continues
Towards the appropriate
Side surely see the
Appearance of the casa
Can't wait even the bangles
I feel to wore them to be
A member yet of the rules
That are harsh to one
Who pays no heed
Maa culture to the
World I feel so touching
So connection coming
As if am a member of maa Composed by Tibez Albershile

24. Val

"Val"

Long a waited From days to weeks
Soon we are approaching
The deed day what we
Gonna do to us
Who luck Skylark
The lonely lord
Can be our witness
Worrying state
To hear indeed
Mi amigos contigo Skylark only Tibez
So sorry indeed
No more of valentine's
Suprise so touching
Indeed tell me
Something so
I can feel feliz
For little a while
Why now all this
Memories melodies
I recall two days
What happened
It's over all my love
I left to a statue
Why all my love
Fade to only was
Work of imagination Indeed was a touching Message making
Tibez to tense I never had of Nor thought of
The deed day
We feel to be fed

With love but
What who feel us
With love now let's
Disfruta mi amigos
Who lack la novia
With our potry world Writing creative world
We believe we gonna
Enjoy to fullest unliken
Those who gonna go
To feel free with
Alcohol con la novia
Let's impress our Day in deed day
To our lovers
Tell them sweet words
Call amor tell Skylark
With sweet melodies
Voice focus on Amor
Face for eternity bond
Tell Skylark swet word Make her feel paradise
Next to you let her go
To field collect bouquet
Of flowers for love
Suprise with many regalo
From the unexpected
So to feel indeed love Make her see the day
She indeed waited
Was not for waste
Composed by Tibez Albershile

25. Sunshine

"Sunshine"
I wanna feel feelings,
Mi amor don't fail me,
I wanna taste at least,
First time for while ,
I hear love y read poems,
Yet l don't know love ,
Can't you feed me ,
I really wanna love,
Am tired of games dear,
Days in out l feel,
So lonely dear can't,
You even liar to me,
With hag beb,
I can't really remember,
When l received love,
Maybe my mother love,
Mi world why don't you,
Give me even little laugh,
With love my lovely,
Heart whom l have chosen,
Over millions mi Moonlight,
Don't you see how much l ,
Really care for you,
Can a dai go down,
Without seeing you,
Album mi Amor
I can't imagine life
Without my love my darling,
I better freeze to a statue ,

Leaving mi Amor is granite,
In my life l really ecanta estas,
Mucho mi heart ,
I wanna know love ,
From mi Amor,
They say am freeze,
I don't have love mi,
Amor l really wanna,
Listen to your love,
Knowledge to my key,
Of my life my bird l ,
Wiii be your learner con ,
Esta world mi Amor,
Composed by Tibez Albershile
Dedicated to my Amor..... Nuevo

26. Wedeo

"wedeo"

Madre you daughter
Esta aqui for long
Time since we
Longed to see
Her indeed am
Lark hoy from
The look of face
Can tell Madre
Madre Madre
Julia and John
Are to marry
More surprising
I nuncar thought of
Yet young primarital son
Was available all
The issues in past
I wonder wiii
Marriage take place
I thought the abortion
Was to led to divorce
Madre more more
Touching to see
Music music
Stage music
The aroma is from
The kitchen is keeping
Me lose my words
The resplendent dress
The hair imported from West island worries me

What gonna take place
We see from far end Make many arrangements
Madre madre
Daughter of her son
Gonna go away
Estas muy cansado
But what we gonna do
See the la novio con his
Padre and abuelo
The dai gonna be big
Baile wiii make me
Laugh yet l have no lover
Let me see the la novia Taking advice of the abuelo
Feliz journey de Encanta
Composed by Tibez Albershile

27. Imagination

" Imagination"

When I woke up l think about anything a part from you

When l imagine of your beautiful night l become

Naughty without knowing possibility of your nature

When I little close my eyes only l see your images

Moving a step a head l see that am holding tight from morning till night

I failed down almost damaging my face

I wonder just memories melodies may lead to

My downfall l can't control myself

Actually it's a bad satution am seeing and experiencing

I thought of l would have any effect of event that passed away years

I have tried to find finest phrase to describe love

All of them go in vain l thought of making it meaningless

The more l describe it l see it in negative nature

Even my attitude and attention is almost winding up

That why l am left helpless in terms of describing it

Simply it was seen as simple so understanding but

Things changed as chameleon changes its colours

Wow wow today am loyal and dedicated but next day am lonely and sorrow

Composed by Albert nyangaresi

28. Relationship

"Relationship"

Love what do we have for today day time , Am looking for ,my schedule if am free that is nice, Am busy as bee ,actually l can't manage love ,

Surely the way l thought ,of sharing moments together,

It's okay but we have to respond to duties ,the relationship follow,

Okay l forgot about it, love l thought today being holiday you are also free,

But it's okay progress, am here am not on any duty today, Okay love, so sorry to know sweet betrayal day time,

What am l not seeing, surely this is work where she said ,

Let l remain calm ,as dead since if l say anything my, results to conflict let l be careful,

Since l don't ,think where our love story by heading to,

Sure because of fame, l can't do nothing to her cheek,

Better to come with permanent solution ,to my satution today

I entered the love story, because of her sweet words

Today l don't know, even meaning of relationship,

I have tried to define, even word relationship ,it's like l have forgot on reality,

Of relationship l wish to spend, relationship with my heavenly father forever,

This age relationship i,s so worrying only money run world of love,

Better to summon my friends, and tell all what l have faced,

In definition of relationship ,the way l was loyal as sand of sea and today am lonely,

Can't believe surely, relationship is all lost ,of time in my daily basis,

Relationship are there but, better to run away from them,

Composed by Albert Nyangaresi

What a day

No sign from my love am lonely as laundry
Why what has happened to me today am dormant volcano
So sorry to me I don't know what I gonna say
All are watching what am experiencing in my today
No one knows about my tomorrow on this love story
Wiii all factors remain the same as past before all has happened
I have no answer to this actually the more I think
The more I lost why the history each time do repeat itself
Am tired I wish to spend my precious time with my love
All that is happening was it written on my destiny
Am worried when Wii I spend sweet moment with my love
Where to erase all barrier that come each day when I feel cross to her
I am not ready to surrender since she is my world
I don't know anyone whom is loyal like her
Why then the mess come up from am worried
Am tired completely with this satution of mine daily basis
Composed by Tiberius Alberto

29. Winner

"Winner"
We may fail to see this due to our mentality,
We can not allow ,virtues to rule our hearts but we allow vices to rule,
We can notbe successful ,winners if we handle our self recklessly,
From your birth you become a winner, why to fail when you know this,
I wonder as wondering, jew just why can not ,we start foreshadowing on our future.
It is so painful being born, winner turning a failure in future,
Be a winner , be a winner set example.
No one dreams such, but our deeds are one determining all this one can not, harvest what he did not plant,
Every mother's wish, is to withness her child becoming winner regardless satution,
Let's start slowly lighting little success tiii we all shine winners
No one gonna stand for you, no body gonna be there,
You gonna be alone , all alone in world of wonders ,
High time to take step, take a chance ,
Make yourself , best bland every ,
Shine tiii , the end of earth everyone to
Chant your name,
Bc a winner , be a winner set example.
Time for the weak it is gone, time for self realisation,
Time for everyone to stand , stand for individuals position,
Time to make world , to recognise our victory,
Born poor does , not limit you to poverty,
Stand up, shine use the ability, use your gift,
It is special believe me,no one is best than you,
You are winner , winner for the world
Be a winner , be a winner set example.

Composed by@ Albert Nyangaresi @Alberto Kelly

30. Time

"Time"
From days to week
Step by step with my
Heart next to me
Weeks to months
Sharing so eternal bond
Thinking of nobody
With your love beb
I see myself paradise
No gaze work you
Are my universe
Months to year
Our love stiii firm
As if it was yesterday
I just see my Skylark
Yet year is down the line
I can't imagine like image
Why million questions
Day in out yet you
Are my only one
Arent you confident
With mc mi amor
Time has gone surely
Am a jew entire anos
Hoy mi trust isnt there
Touching story of to say
Many more cute cunning
Arent in my heart
My only heart is hurry
To hurt me to tears

Take my keys and password
Of my heart but never hurt me
Am a magnetic in your world
Better to be a slave
Of my heart surely
That myself to be pieces
My peace is importante
Mi amor mi encanta
Tu eres Tibez encanta
Tu estas mucho mi heart
Composed by Tibez Albershile
Dedicated to mi Amor

31. Sorrow

"Sorrow "

Where when and whom to start, with who to finish with,

I am helpless and hopeless , My friends and family close friends are mocking me by my decision,

Why can I hide my face ,from facing the reality,

The same Skylark , same moonlight ,

Today what to say , when people hear,

My sweetheart ,is stoning me directly l wonder why,

Yet am so simple as Job, in holy scripture ,

My sweet stories ,are not anymore my love it is over ,

I never thought of, l am speechless seeing satution,

My life has changed, as chameleon changes it is colours,

I am brain storming ,yet to know solution to sad story,

My title soon is winding up as wild, that are hunt daily basis,

Whom gonna listen ,to my stories who gonna love me ,

My heart is hurt , so sad to say to universe to see, So sorry to narrate to audience , the betrayal of love,

Whom gonna be with me, hold my hands and say eternity,

Whom gonna journey , with me this dark phase of mine,

Who gonna say l love you, once again for real,

For sure are many , questions yet cero answers

Composed by Albert nyangaresi

32. Situation

"Situation"

My today ,my tomorrow is a Mistry,

My life is full of , questions and no answers to them,

Mind is tired of this, when wiii it be over,

Am completely worried ,why me after all what is ,

My mistake why to ,go through such satution,

Am helpless no one, to call for help up and down only l and myself ,

I thought of l had loyal friend ,where when did they flew away, I can not tell l can not,believe what did, l do wrong to them, l found no answer,

Only l leave almighty Allah, whom can answer me all the questions,

Sure l wiii keep on fighting ,since he is all knowing,

When l to receive the,when my friends to receive,

When to shower is gratitude, is to him only l is to wait and watch his blessings, My life is surely meangless, without him what am today and what am planning to be tomorrow is to him,

Am greatful that ,is not selfish since l do not know what l could have been saying today,

Fear him let you heart ,be feeled with his great deeds .

Composed by Tibez albershile

33. Political

"Political"

Where are they ,with their promises,

I am worried, my mind is not calm at all,

I am helpless seeing ,what is the satution today,

Their false promises ,make me fail to understand,

What and when ,people see the reality,

When wiii people vote ,wisely for leaders,

Corruption is dorminating, continues as disease,

Yet we all have better, solution for satution.

When , whom gonna put the corrupted official behind bars,

What suprise me ,is when the court is leading ,

Cases are sent, but since of poverty you lose for the high class,

Where wiii we get justice ,for sure so shameful,

Current condition, is calling for help from outside ,

I am withnessing, without anything to say to comment,

The living standard is high, yet high class can't see ,

They are ready to snatch ,everything even a single cent,

So sorry to see such ,painful ruling in the republic.

Where are we going to hide ,our eyes from seeing ,

The evils that is conducted by this current class of ruler's,

Am worried why ,did we waste our vote to vote ,

Where is the work ,to us when you are qualified yet you are denied while some from their ascent is given,

When wiii we mature, we leave tribalism as culture we progress particularly ,

What is the meaning, of education if it ends up to nothing ,

So painful to say, that you are in an independent nation while full of natives.

Composed by Albert nyangaresi

34. Medeo

"medio"

Call her my cure
To my life time
Areadly am gone
I only wanna see
My doctor day
By day doing
Her duties to
Me no more
Just her and her
Talk of her and her
I wiii add more
Hours for her
Talk her bad
Cut my minutes
She is my antidote
My troubles are over
Just by look of her
Am paradise
Whom wiii
Call mi medio
Para mi estas
Muy cansado
Hablamous to
Me when where
I gonna go
Just to see her
Seek her scent
Am exhausted of
The other patient

I see my journey With joan just
We start jokely
Is heading to heavenly
Rout no more of them
Me and you you in me
Tibez in you your
Bonito es one in million
Mi medio mi medio
Cant wait why all
The waiting for
Composed by Tibez Albershile

35. Madre

"Madre"
Winner to world
Who doesn't know
Nothing amazing like
This having winner Madre is my winner
I will not listen to anything
My teacher my friend
How can l forget that
My good influencer
She always supports me
Step by step call her my
Angel guardian
I gain dinero or not
You are my madre
No one gonna get
Your place in my life
Days may go also
Years you wiii
Still be my madre
Many may try
To influence me to
Erase you in my
Success story
Yet you wiii be my
Light to lit me
Erasing light
Is so complex
Count your downfall
My madre l ecanta
Estas mucho mi amigo My maestro en various

Leavel con esta life
You influence millions
Direct or indirect in
Our today tomorrow
Decision depends on
Our upbringing
Moral and maturity
Make everyone say
Indeed esta hijos
Esta muy bueno
Madre continue con
Your bueno heart to Teach and time wiii
Reward you where
You deserve l can't
Denny it and indeed
Our God is indeed
Loving and caring So you gonna stay
Tiii ripe for fruits
Of your hard work Madre indeed I am
Left with no word to
Hablamous gracias Composed by Tibez Albershile

36. Worries

" Worries"
I worry as I wonder
Just as l worry what to say
Where to secure secret answers
Where did l lost my loyal lovely beb
When did l even l missed his missed call even once
Where to trace her when imposter are many
Mostly are mindful
They are imagine of how to know you secret with me
They even can't trace where we knew each other
They think they are replacing you as a ring
No one can take you from my heart
Years have passed since I heard from you
I wonder if the imposter imposed a barrier for you
I don't know what happened l know nature wiii do something to bring us back eliminating the divisioner
I wonder why the imposter came from
Thinking of using your name l can't be able to know you
No matter how much her efforts be she can't be like you my lovely lively Liz
East West of earth l wiii trace you
I hope and happily know that l wiii definitely found you for you are my forever
I don't need anyone a part from you my missing part of my heart
I real miss you together with you melodies voice
Composed by Albert nyangaresi

37. Wonder

"Wonder "
Actually l have been awaked by her love
The sweet scent has made me smile
So sweet melodies sounds from my sugar as made me a statue
I wanna speak Milion words but am speechless
She has taken my heart yet a tender age
I wonder where l gonna start to say this
Actually am wondering as wondering jew on July
I wish to see her each moment but many things act as barrier
I am worried of losing her since she is my world
She knows many stories that make me smile a little
Simplicity is her style of living
So small so humbled my little angel that l adore
Actually l love her alot l wanna call her name numerous times
Sweet name Jane that mark my love story
Actually l am addict to your love
Composed by Tibez Albershile

38. Poverty

" Poverty"
Sunlight again ,
Dawn again but no gain, trying my best to see no pain ,
Still tired to pervert chain,
Tears down like chain,
Pours down like rain,
Sunset,it is nouche nothing to gain So sorry , what to tell my beloved,
My entire day,no gain my efforts,
Went to vain , so touching to say,
What children, family wii get,
Only questions, without answes,
My grace of almighty, shower me,
With something, what wiii my
Parents have, wiii l sell again,
Nouche is approaching,
The birds are singing, my love,
Waiting for husband, today we,
Gonna get something, indeed my child,
Nothing in hands , what is this ,
Again nothing , nothing ,
What a foolish husband,
What wiii parents have , my wife calm,
My father is sick, yet nothing,
Don't say it , you gonna stay ,
Outside hoy tiii you, know the value,
Of being a man , man man ,
Am tired am tired,l wish to end ,
My life l try , my best yet no one,
See that my efforts, goes empty,
Why God , why me each day ,

My hardship work , my Skylark,
See nothing , dawn to down ,
What a satution ,whom gonna elaborate,
My state for me, my status is wanting,
Each day , every minute my mind,
Gonna evaporate , let me count my
Minutes ,my life is done day time,
Composed by Tibez Albershile
Ft @lamsylay

39. Way

"Way"

My mind is full of thought for many things am watching

Almighty God granted success to us as gift

Why we can't see it we aren't going toward right path We aren't focused about what we are going to face

Our negative vices are going to take us to sin

My satution today am helpless where to start where to finish

Mi first and true friend is on dark on day time

Why can we allow thiny success make us sin

That makes me to worry a lot my only true friend

We have allowed our hearts to be filled by our lust which results to lose

Your commitment going in vain in various parts

So painful to guide a person who is completely lost

Composed by Albert nyangaresi

40. Sorry

"Sorry"
    Memories melodies,
    Might make my ,
    Mind mad so ,
    Touching to hear,
    The previous love story,
    Young yearning for love,
    Yet so sad to tell ,
    Climax of complete story,
    Maybe was the wiii of ,
    Destiny day in out ,
    Milion more touching,
    Questions,
    My heart l had found,
    Gold of good state,
    From first day l saw her,
    Indeed she was mi Moonlight,
    Yet my nature didn't consider,
    She thought me definition of love,
    Yet that love made me laugh her,
    Why this when it really happend,
    Speed in seconds ,
    Changed everything my Skylark ,
    Is of existing mind wiii be erased,
    What is value of cellular,
    Can cellular get me her,
    Am worried why all,
    Nor advice l heed from amigos,
    I really was chameleon,
    So sad to say it's climax,

She predged particularly to ,
Our love story but all went,
In vain nor did l listen ,
To her story or her message,
I really wonder if sorry ,
Can have impact to her,
My heart mi Amor,
Melodies may kill Tibez,
No day no time ,
I can be free from,
Recalling our memories,
Just from start of our love
Journey jointly l saw joan,
You were my world,
Yet today l only have word,
When wiii thing get to righful ,
Place only is my brain storming,
My sunshine she had thought me,
Many million things yet hoy ,
Nothing is there .
Composed by Tibez Albershile

41. Measure

"Measure"
Our day, deeds
Are counted continuesly
Good or bad get ready
So touching to see
Our father isn't mean
He always shows us
Path to follow for
Our future decision
My heart is hurt
To see and tell
Indeed Jah deeds
Are amazing
No one no time
His deed Can be bad
He does everything in earth
To give certain message
From start of this journey joy
Was seen but soon
Dark page wiii be waiting
To be seen in the family
No man can change
Destiny with dinero
Sin dinero only searching
Christ can make impossible possible We don't know our fate fear
Almighty first and rest wiii
Follow for this is indeed
A warning for one born
Must day one day
How wiii everything remain

The bread winner best husband
Loving caring husband
But no one can erase
What was already written
Only we can pray particularly
To father for his wiii be done
Fear fear fast furious
Dark phase is coming
Be careful con your deed
Since no man is perfect
Nor our bodies permanent
For this be a person who Does each day measures
Your deed dont wait The climax is clearly
Coming from far
No one is speared
Day in dedicated
Your life to Lord
Composed by Tibez Albershile

The end.

POETRY DE ENCANTA

www.ingramcontent.com/pod-product-compliance
Lightning Source LLC
Chambersburg PA
CBHW060456160726
47992CB00003B/1231